M000028496

THE GOD PARTICLE

MERCER UNIVERSITY PRESS

Endowed by

TOM WATSON BROWN
and
THE WATSON-BROWN FOUNDATION, INC.

THE GOD PARTICLE

God–Talk in A "Big Bang" World

R. Kirby Godsey

MERCER UNIVERSITY PRESS | *Macon, Georgia*

2016

MUP/ H919

© 2016 by Mercer University Press
Published by Mercer University Press
1501 Mercer University Drive
Macon, Georgia 31207

9 8 7 6 5 4 3 2 1

Books published by Mercer University Press are printed
on acid-free paper that meets the requirements of the
American National Standard for Information
Sciences—Permanence of Paper for Printed Library
Materials.

ISBN   978-0-88146-585-3
Cataloging-in-Publication Data is available from the
Library of Congress

.

Dedicated
To

The Mountain Top Lectures

A Forum for Nurturing
Thoughtful Believers

CONTENTS

PREFACE

Aristotle observed that all persons, by nature, desire to know. Science represents a towering achievement of human beings in their search for knowledge. The power of the human mind and the use of our intellectual capacity to understand the world in which we are living has fueled scientific discoveries and has been and continues to be a major force in advancing human civilization. We should eagerly embrace the powers of scientific analysis and the robust regimes of experimentation and observation that science offers us. Science is making our world a better and safer place to live.

To be sure, our scientific achievements, like other human achievements, can be used for unholy and destructive purposes. Nuclear energy cannot only light homes, it can annihilate whole nations. The tools made possible by scientific advance not only build combines to expedite harvests, they also build better tanks to expedite wars. The power of flight introduced to us by the Wright brothers that enables millions to traverse our globe daily, also carries bombs to distant targets with both stealth and precision. The human challenge is to push forward the advances of science, while managing the destructive outcomes that those advances inevitably foster.

Religion, too, is embedded deeply in the human experience. Humankind has a long history of diverse religious affirmations. Religion is viewed by some as a pre-scientific phenomenon. For those individuals, the religious instinct has been effectively supplanted by scientific progress. I suspect that the proclamations of the demise of religion are premature. While the landscape of religious institutions is changing, just as are the territories of science, both science and religion will continue to remain dominant forces within our lives.

Clearly, just as scientific advances can be used for unholy purposes, religious abuses have also become far too common. Religion has been used as a justification for unthinkable atrocities. It is being used to suppress the advance of women in a world that has been mostly ruled by men. Religion is being used as a defense for prejudice against gays and lesbians, just as it was used to defer addressing social injustices against blacks and other minorities. The abuses of both science and religion are abundant throughout human history, but, in recent decades, the destructive capacity of both have escalated dramatically.

Even so, both science and religion have been and remain major and important enablers of the progress of human civilization. They together continue to bring critical resources to cope with our complex human situations. It is sheer folly when religion seeks to diminish the power and the progress brought about by scientific inquiries. Similarly, science should not seek to diminish the powerful role that religion plays in advancing human understanding and inspiring people to live more noble and caring lives. While guarding against and becoming more explicit and aggressive in calling out the abuses of both science and religion, we should underscore that the human course of progress, our yearning for hope and peace, will be best achieved through conversations and cooperation, not through demonization and exclusivity.

In the essays that follow, I am advocating that we should learn from the important advances of science, and recognize that these advances can helpfully inform our conversations about faith. Religious truth and scientific truth are ultimately coherent. It is not constructive for faithful believers to engage in religious dogma that runs counter to what we are learning about our world. To the contrary, while we are learning from science, we should explore avenues of belief that take into account the knowledge we are gaining about our amazing world. Religions too must be willing to change their theological propositions. Not all revelation is past tense. It is possible for religion and science to grow by listening and learning from one another.

In the final analysis, I believe that our universe with all its diversity shares a transcendent oneness, a unity which should inform all our daily work. We need the knowledge that science is continually expanding. We also need the insights that enrich our lives from a host of poets and prophets who enlighten our understanding of living in our world.

This book is based upon lectures presented in the Mountain Top Lectures in Amicalola Falls, Georgia. I am grateful to Bill Saling and David Griffin and the engaging audience who attended these lectures. Their leadership and their conversations benefited immensely my efforts to promote continuing discussions among people who love the study of cosmology and theology.

I want to express my appreciation for the editorial commentary and counsel of my daughter Stephanie Shepherd. Her questions and observations, as well as her grammatical and syntactical suggestions made the text more accurate and precise. My tireless Administrative Assistant, Jeannette Taylor, was responsible for the preparation of the manuscript and, with persistent good spirit, worked through the many textual amendments. My friends and colleagues through many years, Walter and Kay Shurden, read the text in draft form and their comments greatly improved the final text. Conversations with other colleagues and friends, including Don Midkiff, Richard Swindle, Mary Wilder, and Chris Blake have raised questions and added insight and perspective as I wrestled with the issues reflected in these essays. My brother, Jack Godsey, a man of profound insight into the physics of our universe, and I talked on many occasions about the ideas that are prominent in this work. While I take responsibility for all that I have written, I found his understanding of the physics of this vast universe in which we reside to be both informative and inspiring.

Finally, I am grateful for the thoughtful guidance of Marc Jolley, the director of Mercer University Press. He convinced me to translate my lectures into a book and served as the editor for the project. His thoughtful reflections and the persistent nudges of his staff, Marsha Luttrell and Mary Beth Kosowski, made possible the timely publication of the book.

I close this brief preface by reminding the reader that he or she is likely to sense that the text was originally spoken. As a result, the idiom and the flow of language is sometimes affected by the engagement with an audience. For me, the highest goal of this work does not lie in any knowledge the text may provide, much less the facts it may illuminate. The highest goal will be achieved in the conversations and the discussions that might be engendered among people who embody very different experiences and perspectives. At the end, this book is mostly a celebration of mystery. We are yet in the infancy of human development and understanding. We will learn and grow by listening to one another, by seeking to transcend our own histories and prejudices, and by attuning ourselves more fully to the wisdom of the universe.

THE GOD PARTICLE

I.

ROMANCING THE UNKNOWN

Both theology and cosmology begin with the siren call of mystery. We live in a cloud of unknowing. This absence of knowing is different from ignorance. Ignorance is the failure to exercise our capacity to know the known. The cloud of unknowing springs from the awareness that all of our knowledge, scientific, philosophical, and religious, leads us back to a sea of the unknown to which we also belong. The inexplicable in your life and mine trumps what we can explain. That is our persistent human condition. Scientists and theologians, philosophers and cosmologists are engaged in an epistemological dance, romancing the unknown.

In its most daring moments, science lifts the veil of mystery ever so slightly. Even so, scientists are first in line to declare that what we do not know greatly exceeds what we do know. The mystery courses through our veins and the veins of every blazing galaxy.

Closer to where we live, it often takes a lifetime to discern the mystery of our essential interconnectedness with one another and our own creative connectivity to all that exists within our universe. Focusing on our vast and complex world, the question may arise, "Is life about anything more than living until we die?"

Human beings are often threatened by the boundary of death. It does feel like a final frontier, a point of no return toward which we are hurtling. We are equally threatened, I believe, by the boundary of another person. Other people are so elusive. We often cannot get a grip on another person's inner thoughts. We cannot see the secret places in their minds and their hearts. That inability to control another person's thoughts can generate fear, and that fear sometimes leads to terrible episodes of abuse. The shadows of the unknown make us feel uneasy.

The first and the second essays are about some of what science has learned from observing our mysterious world and science's efforts to decipher the cosmic code. The essays that follow the first and the second are about faith's efforts to speak of the ultimate mystery, necessarily employing the power of myth and poetry. The concluding essays are about embracing the mystery of relatedness and our essential interdependence as an enlightening clue for living our lives.

Relatedness or, if I could coin a word, "relationality" turns out to be among our most telling ciphers for understanding the creative energy that is fashioning our universe. All living beings are cousins. Everything is related. In science, "fields" may be thought of as relational. Fields are not discrete things. They are spread out. You and I are "spread out" as well. In human terms, the field of our being is the interrelatedness that characterizes our being present. You and I live in the human field of being. The lone, unrelated individual is sheer fiction.

There are two kinds of mystery—one refers to what is "not-yet known." Exploring the region of the "not-yet-known" is the territory of scientific study, of historical and archeological and genetic explorations. We are continually and wisely pushing back the boundaries of the "not-yet-known." We have a mighty long way to go. We are, in fact, barely in the crawling stage. We should add that we have learned more in the last 100 years than was known in all of human history before.

The second kind of mystery is the kind posed by Martin Heidegger and others—Leibniz, for example—in the question: "why is there something rather than nothing?" That question frames the mystery to which you and I also belong. That mystery is not outside us. The mystery courses through us. Why are we here? That question is not mostly a scientific question; it is a theological question that science can perhaps be helpful in framing the answer. Yet, we are not likely to travel far enough in space or find enough elementary particles or examine enough x-rays to answer that question.

As we reflect upon the nature and character of our lives, the discussions that follow will suggest that you and I are not best described as discrete objects. Each of us is a self with integrity and genuine individuality, but we are not independent, self-contained objects. We are entirely interdependent. Each of us is an ascending wave in an infinite sea of interrelated being. The notion that the spiritual and the material are different zones of reality fades away as we learn that we and everything else in the universe are connected. Mind and spirit, like matter and energy, are simply different manifestations of our being.

We could simply speak of the ultimate mystery as God, but in our language, the use of the name God is our first step toward demystifying and controlling the mystery. It would be better not to speak of God at all than to think that we can control the transcendent mystery we call God. We can never fully rationalize this cloud of unknowing. We have to learn from the poet and give in to the wonderfully revealing resources of myth and metaphor. When it comes to speaking of God, music may be more powerful than words.

Both scientism, which believes there is no mystery beyond the not-yet-known, and religious fundamentalism, which believes there is no mystery because we have all the answers in our religious dogma, are reductionist approaches to understanding our world. For scientism, the world is the sum total of what is known and what is yet to be known. What we know and can know is all there is. Religious fundamentalism, whether Christian or Muslim or Jewish or Hindu, does away with mystery by offering a set of faith affirmations that should be believed as life's ultimate explanations. Most scientists are not victims of scientism, and most religious people are not victims of fundamentalism. But those forms of religion and science abhor uncertainty. I gladly embrace uncertainty. I believe it is by finding the courage to dwell in the land of uncertainty that we really are most likely to be surprised by the voice of God.

Whether we refer to the mystery as the Eternal Word, or the unknown Logos that floods through the universe, or the God beyond our gods, or the Inner Light, there is an uncertain field of mystery that is the final reality that we all embody. You and I are the mystery made flesh.

II.

THE GOD PARTICLE

We begin by focusing on the recent advances in understanding the physical nature of the world in which you and I live. Our perceptions are very limited. Our senses have narrow bandwidths. We can see, for example, only a sliver of the wave lengths of light. We are not equipped to see most of the light in the world, gamma rays, for example. We can hear only a very small segment of sound. Most animals have far better hearing and sensory apparatus than we. Whether speaking of gravitational waves or cosmic entanglement or the god particle, our entire being is embedded in the wonder of creative mystery. Our perception and our understanding are very limited.

Seeing through a glass darkly as it were, if we expect to have a sustainable faith, our beliefs and our belief systems need not run counter to what we are actually learning about the world. Let me be plain about one of my bedrock assumptions. Religion is not a surrogate science. The faith we embrace should not call upon us to reject reason, for if we do, reasonable people will ultimately reject faith.

On July 4, 2012, a genuinely historic discovery was announced. This discovery received worldwide attention, namely the announcement of the discovery of the Higgs boson. Though a strange sounding word, in all candor, the Higgs boson was a really dramatic achievement. This elementary element was named for Peter Higgs, a distinguished British physicist who first predicted its existence in the 1960s. The announcement of its discovery drew the attention of youthful inquirers as well as scientists and mathematicians who, for almost 50 years, had been at work on the issue of whether this certain particle existed. There at the nuclear laboratory was an audience of "20-somethings" and "80-somethings" all waiting, like fans at a rock concert, to hear the outcome of the experiments taking place within the Hadron Collider in CERN, a research facility located on the border between Switzerland and France.

A brief word about this Hadron Collider: It is actually called The Large Hadron Collider or "LHC." This machine is 16.7 miles in circumference. It is located about 300 feet underground and cost almost $10 billion to build. The word Hadron refers to heavy subatomic particles such as protons. Collider refers to what they do with these particles at very high speeds, and "large" simply refers to the massiveness of this machine—larger than any machine ever built.

The United States had planned to build its own Collider, called the Super Conducting Super Collider, but funding was cancelled by the U.S. Congress in 1993. To the world's good fortune, the Europeans stepped in and constructed the Collider along the border between France and Switzerland. It was turned on for experimentation in 2008. CERN is the European Center for Nuclear Research. The collective research activity at CERN represents 21 countries that govern the operation and contribute most of the budget. Seventy other countries, including the U.S., participate as observers. CERN is a model of international cooperation and is devoted exclusively to peaceful purposes. And Switzerland is a perfect place for this important research because the region is less torn by political and military conflict.

At CERN, the mission is clear: to study the basic constituents of matter and to identify the fundamental building blocks of the universe. The scientists at CERN focus on asking the questions concerning what the universe is made of. What actually constructs this world that you and I live in?

Because religious people have historically relied mostly on myth to describe the origins of the universe, it is important to augment our human understanding by learning from the inquiries of science. Our tools for observing the external world have advanced dramatically. While they, by no means, need to diminish the relevance of our religious stories, such as the Genesis narratives, they can enable us to see that these stories should not be taken as literal descriptions of our origins or the origins of our world. Our actual creation stories have improved, even though the scientific accounts leave us with an abundance of mystery. We often turn to poetry, parable, and myth to help us discern the mystery of which we are a part. While we engage in science and embrace traditions of faith, we should not confuse the two. Confusing religious stories with science leads to bad religion and bad science.

It is not a denigration of faith to say that science offers us a better factual story of the early beginnings of time than do the Genesis narratives. When faith seeks to nullify the facts, those actions are both misguided and arrogant. Faith should not seek to displace facts or make them to accord with our stories of faith. Our faith may indeed take us beyond the regions of science—the regions where poets and prophets may inspire and enlighten the soul, as science seeks to enlighten the mind. Neither displaces the other and surely people of faith should never eschew the scientist's relentless pursuit to understand the nature of the world in which we are living.

The consuming passion of the nuclear scientists at CERN is to examine the physical conditions that took place billions of years ago. By the use of super conducting magnets, scientists steer beams of sub-atomic particles, in this case protons, and accelerate them to a speed of about 99.99% of the speed of light. After achieving these enormous speeds, the protons are crashed into one another, and out of that "trainwreck," new, heretofore never observed particles become visible. In effect, in the LHC, scientists are seeking to create a miniature "big bang."

Well, let's explore what we are learning. The expanding universe in which we live appears to be a massive collection of objects—suns and moons, planets and galaxies, quasars and black holes, not to speak of the mundane objects, such as tables and chairs, trees and animals that make up our daily lives. You and I belong to an expanding world that existed about 10 billion years before the earth came along. But everything that makes up the earth and everything that emerged upon this earth millions of years after it was formed was there from the beginning of time. An important truth: All that is, always was and always will be. It just wears different clothes. There is a oneness, an interrelatedness, a wholeness to the universe that should not escape us. Eastern religions have generally been more at home with that reality than western religions.

The broad consensus of scientists and physicists is that the universe in which we are living today came into being from an intensely dense state of energy about 13.8 billion years ago, as we earthlings measure time. You and I are indeed radical newcomers to the universe. We arrived, at the earliest, a couple of hundred thousand years ago. Something that might be regarded as an elementary human civilization arrived about 12,000 years ago—a mere fleeting whisper of the time of the universe.

We encounter from time to time people who argue and actually believe that the universe is about 6,000 years old. We should be clear. Such affirmations may be viewed as tenets of faith, but they are not tenets of fact. Creationism is not science; it deserves no credible standing in trying to understand the factual world in which we live. In all candor, I believe that the "young earth theory" is intellectually bankrupt both in science and religion. Religious talk that twists and turns the facts in order to make them conform to ancient scriptures needlessly leads people astray. Creationists wind up distorting our understanding of God and betraying history. In addition, they have to trust that a person will never become a thinking believer.

Ignorance is never a sound foundation for building a strong faith. Ignorant believers are surely as important as the well-educated believers, but making ignorance a tenet of belief does not make it any less ignorant. Holy ignorance is still ignorance.

The purpose of science is to help us push back the shadows of ignorance. The reason that the discovery of the Higgs boson is such a major achievement is that it helps us better understand our earliest origins.

The best evidence is, based on observation, that the vast expanse of this universe came into being with the occurrence of what is called the "big bang." Using terms like "big bang" means that science has its own mythology. The "big bang," unlike the big bangs that we might observe on the 4th of July, was not an explosion in space. It was an explosion of space from an intensely dense field of energy. The so-called "big bang" created space and space is still expanding. Prior to that event, there was neither time nor space.

As humans, we are tempted to ask "where" was this ball of energy and "when" did it happen. We have to use our imagination here. "Whereness" did not exist. There was no "where" before the "big bang." The energy was all the "where" there was. There was also no "when." What was before the "big bang" turns out to be a nonsense question. There was no "before." It is like asking, what is North of the North Pole? "Beforeness" and "whereness" all existed within the intensely dense field of energy. There was no space before the "big bang" and there was no time. The universe at that stage is described simply as a "singularity"—an undifferentiated bundle of energy.

Space and time, then, are not infinite. Time is simply a dimension of space–time, and measuring time enables us to label events in our universe. St. Augustine understood the finiteness of time when he concluded that God created time. I prefer to say that time exists within God. Even so, Augustine wrote: "what did God do before he made heaven and earth?" Augustine said, "God was preparing hell for those who ask such questions."

People of faith are inclined to ask whether this original creative event that the scientists refer to as the "big bang" was a purposeful event. Is there a creator? The language of "purpose" and "creator" is important language that flows naturally out of our human situation and our affirmations of belief. We should not quarrel with assigning such human categories to the ultimate character of the universe as long as we understand that we are using human-oriented language to describe trans-human events. The creative event that scientists describe with one language and theologians with another transcends both scientific and religious description. Both scientist and theologian are taking a leap into sheer mystery. Therefore, the person of faith's use of the language of "creator" is no more inappropriate than the scientist's use of "big bang." Though these languages may be satisfying to the mind or to the heart, we cannot and should not propose that our languages unravel the mystery of the creative event that made possible both our world and us.

Scientists mean by the term "singularity" a radical oneness, bound by neither time nor space. Complexity grew out of simplicity. That oneness or simplicity turns out to be a pure interconnected sea of creative energy. Mystics, poets, and philosophers have often written of our essential interrelated oneness. Every poet senses that something's going on in the world and among us that science cannot tell us about. The composer hears what no one else is hearing. The artist sees what others are not seeing. We live in a world that is teeming with creative energy. Heraclitus who lived 500 years before Jesus wrote: "When you have listened not to me but to the Logos, it is wise to agree that all things are one." Oneness is well-grounded in scientific reality as well.

Atoms were born about 300,000 years after the big bang. Hydrogen and helium atoms began to cling together to form stars millions of years later. The crush of hydrogen and helium created elements such as lithium and beryllium and nitrogen. Creativity continues as the crush of converging elements create new particles. Scientists cannot see what was going on before the birth of stars. They can, however, hear what was going on and most of the evidence of the "big bang" came from echoes of cosmic radiation emanating from the "big bang" itself.

By far, the most common element in our universe is hydrogen, made up of one electron orbiting one proton. The first stars were made up almost entirely of hydrogen and helium. Stars formed out of nebulae, which are gaseous collections of matter. The elements within these large and hot stars colliding together created other elements—iron, carbon, oxygen and the entire periodic table of elements.

Those large stars (1,000 times the mass of our sun) sometimes explode into what are called supernovae. The supernovae spread heavier elements such as carbon and oxygen and silicon and iron and lead throughout the universe. Those elements become the seeds of new suns and new planets. Thousands of suns are being formed every day. The universe is in an unceasing state of creation. Every element that makes up our planet Earth and everything that exists on this planet came from an exploding star. So, in the final analysis, you and I are all made of stardust.

Yet, as we look out into the vastness of our universe, it turns out that all of this vastness when we look up at the night sky is composed of imperceptibly small elements. The bundle of energy from which our universe with its stars and galaxies were born from a simple, undifferentiated singularity. From that creative event came all of the elementary particles that make up our universe today, along with the unified force that spread out to be experienced by us as gravity and electromagnetic force, as well as the weak and strong nuclear forces that function in the nuclei of atoms.

Humans have long been fascinated with the fundamental building blocks that make up our world. We have to go all the way back to the Greek philosopher Democritus (460 B.C.) to trace the discussions of the fundamental building blocks. He came up with the idea that water and air and fire and wood and everything else that exists were composed of "atoms." Atom literally means "uncuttable." So an atom was believed to be the fundamental particle that is indivisible. Now it turns out that Democritus was wrong about atoms. They are not the fundamental building blocks of the universe and they certainly are not indivisible. Atoms are constellations of a menagerie of other more fundamental elements. But Democritus was clearly on the right track. He was simply wrong about the elementary elements.

Science is guided chiefly by experimentation and making mathematical inferences. The scientist reports on what he observes and scientists are becoming more and more informed about what actually exists. Scientific discoveries, whether made by Copernicus or Newton or Einstein are powerfully important. Scientists also reach mathematical conclusions about what should exist, and those conclusions often precede by decades any experimental verification. But their findings always lead to a boundary where they seem to fall silent. The rational leads us to the inexplicable. Scientists, like the rest of us, are in an elaborate dance with the unknown.

That dance brings us to the "god particle." The Higgs boson, known as the "god particle," was an enormously important example of a verification of what was accepted scientifically to be the case almost 50 years before any experimental confirmation of its existence. It was a critical piece of the cosmic code, a missing component of the standard model of physics.

So what is the "god particle?" Well, the "god particle" turns out to be neither god nor a particle. While the Higgs boson was a very important discovery at CERN it has nothing to do with the existence of God. The Higgs boson is fodder neither for the theist nor the atheist.

Leon Lederman, another distinguished Nobel Prize-winning physicist, in order to underscore the significance of this discovery, coined the term "god particle." It was a way of underscoring the significance of this entity, but it was also a brilliant strategy for bringing it to the world's attention. This discovery would not have been perceived as nearly so important, and it was truly important, if the announcement was made that they had finally discovered the Higgs boson which had been predicted almost 50 years earlier. That would have been an esoteric, insider announcement, largely unnoticed. Instead, it became instant news, including the CBS and NBC and ABC and CNN Evening News and major news publications such as *Time* and *Newsweek*, where it was announced that a "god particle" had actually been discovered. The discovery, by any measure, was monumental. The name "god particle" was assigned to it in order, in part, to get the world's attention—which it did.

While neither a particle nor God, the Higgs boson confirmed how things, or what I prefer to call events, such as electrons and protons come to have mass. Without mass, we would not have stars or suns or galaxies or people. Massless particles would move at the speed of light. In a world where electrons were without mass, there would be no atoms because electrons would never slow down to bind with nuclei. The Higgs boson pervades all space. The entire universe is suffused in the Higgs field, and by passing through that field, particles gain mass. So the discovery of the Higgs boson was a fundamental building block for understanding the actual origin of things.

For our purposes, what is more basic and I think more interesting than the fact that the Higgs boson is not God is that the "god particle" is also not a particle. And that reality can tell us a lot about ourselves. What we perceive as particles are really "vibrations" in the fields that pervade all space. Most importantly, the Higgs boson is not a particle; it is a field. Furthermore, it turns out that the world, as nuclear physicists make clear, is not a collection of independent particles or objects but a collection of fields. As Sean Carroll, Research Professor of Physics at the California Institute of Technology observed, "Every particle that we know about is actually a field of one kind or another."

Fields constitute the fabric of the universe. Fields are not things or particles related; fields are the universal relatedness from which things or particles are extrapolations. There are no "things" in the world, whether they be electrons, or bosons, or persons, or gods. We describe our interacting with the "fabric fields" as electrons or persons or gods. These names, however, are metaphorical, or in religious language mythological, references to our experiencing the fields of being. A boson is really a field. A person is also a field. Fields, connectedness, relationality will become, I believe, better metaphors for speaking of God. This basic reformation of our thinking, which as I will describe later is sometimes made more difficult by our language, enables us to embrace more fully the advances of science, while being able to achieve a clearer self-understanding. Moreover, in our god-language, this shift in thinking about our world enables us to embrace the power and insight of religious mythology that has suffered from our futile efforts to convert our religious stories that can inspire us into historical and scientific facts.

What we perceive as objects, whether they be stars or atoms or persons, might be better described as congealed or captured energy. Energy is not a locatable entity to be put somewhere. It can be observed, but not located in a discrete space. The "where" of the electron was not there before you looked at it. Your looking at it created the "where". In a sense, your looking at me creates the "me" you see. I am actually a field of congealed energy, a constellation of relationships, and so are you. I noted in my Mountain Top Lectures that Don Midkiff and I have been closest friends for almost 50 years. So, if you do not know my relationship with Don, you do not know me fully. But it is not only your connection with someone you love close up. It is also true of meeting a stranger. Kindness is a way of relating, a way of meeting. Fear and hatred are also ways of relating. Relating kindly changes who you are. Relating hatefully also changes who you are. None of us is a lone individual. Our lives are profoundly interconnected. We belong to a common field of being.

We are beginning to get closer to understanding the world in which we live. We are learning that the world is not a collection of thing-like objects at all. The world is made up of quantum fields, vibrating in every location and throughout time. What we call particles are what we see when we look at those fields. A particle is simply the quantizing of a field. Everything in the universe, including you and me, is ultimately more like a field than an object.

III.

VERBS AND HYPHENS: SYMBOLS OF RELATEDNESS

For convenience of speaking, we might divide our world into different strata. We will call the universe writ large the "macro-strata," made up of suns and galaxies, of black holes and nebulae, some of which we can observe with our eyes and our earth-based telescopes, and some of which we are deploying satellites and orbiting telescopes to explore more distant regions. There is also the universe writ small which we can call the "micro-strata." It is composed of atoms and molecules and even smaller elements such as protons and neutrons and electrons, quarks and gluons. There is yet another strata that perhaps interests us most because it is the world written on a human scale. We might call this strata the meso (meaning middle)-strata. It is the universe of people and trees and mountains and tables and chairs with which we interact. That's where we live.

What these three diverse strata—galaxies, (macro) electrons (micro), and people (meso)—hold in common is that none is, in its essence, constellations of things.

Galaxies, electrons, and people are more like events than objects. We are more like dynamic happenings than static entities. We and everything in the world are fields of relatedness. By relatedness, I do not refer to things existing independently of being related. Rather, relatedness or relationality is the reality underlying all things, whether they be stars or electrons or persons. Entities are an extrapolation from the field of relatedness. Like the "macro" and the "micro" world, the world on a human scale turns out to be a vibrating field of interconnectedness.

Learning to think of ourselves as extrapolations from a field of relatedness helps us begin to understand that the universe, including you and me, as I like to say, is far more like a verb than a noun. Yet our language and our identities are dominated by nouns. He is a chef. He is a pilot. She is an engineer. He is a teacher. We call people "nouns." Of course, people are not really nouns; they are closer to being verbs. God is not a noun sitting somewhere out there; God is a verb, moving among us. You are not a thing; you are an event. Behind our handy nouns, in every case, there is a teeming reality that resists being confined by a name. Nouns, however, are the linguistic cards we have been dealt. So we are not going to stop using them, whether we are speaking of a proton or a person or God. But we need to take their "nounness" less seriously.

As we speak more precisely, the universe, including the meso-strata of reality, is not a collection of independent, self-contained entities at all. You and I are episodes of light. We are events. We are constellations of connectivity. We are embodied energy.

The notion of people and things as substantive objects is figurative language, a convenient fiction. It is a useful fiction, but fiction nonetheless.

Seeing ourselves as people in the making, emerging from the reality of that ultimate bundle of energy, beyond which there is only transcendent mystery, is the essence of our being here. It is not just the source of our being here; it is the essence of our being here. We are not bobbing adrift as isolated individuals disconnected from this sea of creative energy. We are intrinsically connected. These realities mean that the traditional way of conceiving God no longer works. Either God does not exist or she is very different from what we thought.

Every one of us is scientifically, ontologically, and theologically related to everything else. Every star is a creative event. Every person is a "starry" episode participating in the same creative mystery that forms the stars. And like the star we call our sun, we will, like our sun, change forms, but the creative being that is our essence will never dissipate.

At the intersection of science and religion, science is sometimes accused of causing some people to lose their religion. I suspect, however, that religion, more than science, has been the chief cause of people losing their religion. Bad religion perennially turns out to be the chief cause of no religion. The problem is not that people's religion is taken from them. To the contrary, people sometimes eagerly throw their religion overboard because they find it to be an unreasonable appendage for a reasonable person.

I am a Baptist. It may take 20 years to grow a Baptist and 20 minutes to lose one to no religion at all. It happens when a person cannot make his religion square with what else he knows. Who among us has not from time to time (it can be a repetitive episode), shaken his or her head in disbelief? For example, and being personal, I can recall at times, avoiding church on Easter Sunday. It is not because I thought the resurrection was not a relevant and rich idea or experience. It was because I found it dispiriting and disrupting of faith to listen to homilies built around an effort to establish and to defend the historical validity of the resurrection of Jesus. The fact is that we know very little about Jesus as a historical figure and we know even less about the resurrection. The fact of the resurrection may be an interesting, even intriguing debate, but that issue will not be resolved as a factual or historical issue. The resurrection cannot be established as a historical fact.

Insofar as science or cosmology or critical thinking and analysis causes us to doubt some of our religious beliefs, it is likely that those beliefs deserve to be doubted. Our duffle bags of certainties in religious beliefs are far too large. We would do well to trade in our large duffle bags for smaller briefcases. Through the years, my satchel of certainties has diminished in size. I have learned that truth cannot be equated with certainty. If our consuming desire is to find reliable facts, we are more likely to find them in the catacombs of science. The catacombs of faith are not rich in facts; they are rich in helping us come to terms with what on earth we are doing here.

We should acknowledge that science can account for the universe or even the mathematical possibility of multiverses and parallel universes without reference to God. It is not the business of science to discover either God or the "god particle." It is the business of science to push the boundaries of the not-yet-known as far as they can be pushed. It is also clearly not the mission of science to certify the validity of any religion. And it is surely not the business of religion to become a surrogate science. There are scientists who are profoundly devout, and there are some who come to rest in some form of agnosticism—not knowing. Science is not a firm foundation for either theism or atheism. On the other hand, if our religion becomes a substitute for science, it will likely lead to a failure of faith.

I suppose that we learned from Adam, not science, to "name" things. Adam may be the culprit. Naming things is quintessentially human. Apparently, we are the only known beings that name things. When we name something, as I said earlier, we "noun" it. We give it a place and time. It is called "control." We nail it down. We corral it. The problem with naming or "nouning" a child or a boson is that we can never quite corral it. It will not stay in place. Electrons are not good at staying in place. And children, especially, are not good at staying in place. That is because, please remember, they are not nouns at all.

Science and religion, cosmology and theology converge in the realization that nothing is a noun because self-sustaining things do not exist in the world. You and I turn out to be sheer connectivity. You are a part of me and I am a part of you. Alfred North Whitehead was right when he said that thinking of "things" as concrete objects is "misplaced concreteness." Our being lies in the "between," not in the extrapolation we call an individual. Everything is connected.

In Martin Buber's I-Thou, it is not I *and* Thou. It is I-Thou. The "hyphen," the between, is the operative symbol, not the "and." The "I" exists solely in relation to the "Thou" and the "Thou" exists solely in relation to the "I." This ground of connectedness is our clearest manifestation of God. We live hyphenated existences. If we are to find God, we will likely find God in the hyphens of our lives.

This means that every person is a person in the making. You are not a localized object. You and I are hyphenated fragments of stardust. We are hyphenated fragments of light penetrating the world.

Because we are awed by the magnitude and vastness of the universe, we have plenty of room for both scientific and theological humility. We have barely lifted the veil. We know so little. But we are learning more every day. Scientists are becoming more effective in observing, such as our flyby of Pluto and the discovery of Kepler 452b, a planet that exists in the "goldilocks" zone of its sun that is 1,400 light-years away. Yet this vast and captivating universe is now acknowledged by nuclear physicists and astrophysicists to make up less than 5% of our universe. About 27% of the universe is estimated to be dark matter, and 68% of the universe is estimated to be made up of dark energy, neither of which we have ever seen or observed. We know nothing, then, about 95% of the universe. We refer to dark energy and dark matter because we are scientifically "in the dark" about the nature of these phenomena. We simply know they exist. It is one more piece of evidence that most of the universe belongs to the not-yet-known.

In the next essay, I will suggest how we have to reform our God talk. We must use the power of myth in a world where objective things do not really exist and a world in which mystery outranks knowledge.

Moving beyond defining ourselves as objects means that each of us would be better described as a "region of behavior." You and I are not simply collections of blood, muscle, and bone. We are emerging as the universe is emerging. To know you, I must not simply know your height and weight and the color of your eyes. I must know about the interrelatedness that creates your being here. I must know people who are a part of your soul. Energy and thought and creativity are embodied in every individual self.

When it comes to the noun, "god," I suspect that God is most clearly, though not exclusively, encountered and known in meeting one another. Strictly speaking, God as a noun does not exist. God as a being that you can set aside in a corner of our crazy world does not likely exist. Every person and every star is an expression of the Godness beyond our gods that resides within each of us and within every star, yet transcends all our existence.

Neither theism nor atheism may be dishonorable views of God. Both viewpoints may become avenues for experiencing the sacredness of the world in which we live. Unfortunately, both views too often trivialize the notion of God. The theists do so by conceiving God as an object that can be named. And whenever I have asked atheists to tell me about the god they do not believe in, I find that I also do not believe in that god.

The image of God maintains within me, first and foremost, a sense of wonder and an increasing reverence for creation. After earning four doctoral degrees, Albert Schweitzer devoted his entire life to what he called "reverence for life" by caring for forgotten people in a remote corner of the earth. Far more powerful than words, Schweitzer's vocation embodied his deep reverence for life. He did not preach reverence; he lived reverence. For me, all creation is the speaking of God. I stand in awe. I fall in love with the depth and wonder of our world and, for me, the image of God means being captured by a speechless wonder.

When we bow to offer thanks for a meal, we are not thanking an object beyond, we are expressing gratitude for the manifestations of God that are at this very moment sustaining us. Every common meal, in which we are aware of our essential inter-connectedness, our genuine interdependence is an act of holy communion. Each of us, then, like the Higgs boson, might be referred to as a "god parti-cle." The universe is teeming with God. Creation is not past tense. Each one of us is a God fragment in the world. You are God's creative presence made flesh. If you wish to know the sacred, look nearby. God is closer than you may think.

IV

THE BOSON AND OTHER MYTHS OF GOD

Every speaking of God is a myth. When we do not wish to speak of God in mythical terms, we have to resort to silence.

Science writes the lyrics of the universe. Myth provides the music. We should use myth broadly to include poetry and parable, musical interludes, and moving images of God that inspire us. Every religion, then, might be thought of as a song of the universe. They are collections of beautiful myths, stories of fear and hope, stories of failure and success, stories of life and death that keep us going in this weird and uncertain world.

We have to use symbol and metaphor when we come to the limits of rational thought. The people of faith sing about what they cannot see. The scientist, on the other hand, may send a deeper probe to uncover yet unseen territories. But whether scientists or cosmologists, philosophers or people of faiths, we are all reaching for the stars. We are reaching out to touch the untouchable and to see the unseen, or in the words of Immanuel Kant, to probe the "starry heavens above and moral life within." We are reaching to experience the transcendent Nothingness, the "No-Thing-ness," from which we spring. When religion pretends to lay intellectual claim on God, or presumes to have God figured out, that is the first sign of a decaying religion. Faith is never about laying claim. It is more about giving in than laying claim.

You and I will never be able to explain God. Silence is far more telling. The Jews were closer to symbolizing that truth when they would not utter Yahweh's name. In the Jewish tradition, that practice reminds us that God is not to be possessed in our minds or in our words or in our doctrines.

When speaking of God, myth and metaphor are the very best we can do. Religions at war with one another expose the brokenness of our myths. Myths harden into creeds and certainties. Myths become degraded into doctrines to be defended, rather than music and light to inspire us and to help us see. Competing myths are like feuds among children, but they can have very adult consequences. We would not think of using deadly weapons to establish the superiority of Beethoven over Bach. But for some, the differences between the Christian myth and the Islamic myth are deadly serious. The differences are real, but they should not be deadly. Many of the world's religions, including Christianity, have missionary or proselytizing endeavors buoyed by a passion to proclaim their "message" to the "ends of the earth." Bearing witness can be a natural and constructive outcome of religious experience, but it can, and often does, breed arrogance, exclusivity, and even bigotry. If we wish to avoid that devolution, our "proclaiming" must be accompanied with listening and honest conversation. Authentic respect is the best antidote for religious arrogance.

I have believed in the past that the greatest threat to human civilization was the development of nuclear weapons. It is apparent that we humans have developed far more power to destroy than we have the moral insights to manage. Our weapons of destruction are an increasing menace to civilization. Beyond the increasing power of our weapons, killing has become remote and sterile—no human intervention required. I have said in the past that civilization is in a foot race. We are racing to see if our moral discernment can catch up with our human destructive capacity. We have today the ability to completely abolish human life. We have the capacity to turn our earth into one more barren, silent rock in the wilderness of space.

Despite the catapulting deadliness of our weapons, I have more recently come to believe that perhaps the more grave threat to our human civilization lies not in the development of more deadly weapons alone, but also in the narcissism of our human religions. The combination of mightier weapons and bad religion has become the deadliest combination of all. The terror being bred in the name of religious mythologies are a genuine and existential threat to the progress of human civilization. Religion itself, sometimes wearing Christian or Hindu or Islamic clothing, is being turned into killing fields that mock the sacredness of human life. While I live with a spirit of optimism, I cannot be certain that the human race can survive the hubris of power and the evil abuses of religion.

Despite our human threats, the telling of stories and the formation of myths give voice to the wonder of our lives and the awesome world to which we belong. The challenge is that our myths tend to crystalize into immutable belief systems. They breed precise and specific and exclusive plans of salvation and absolute answers to life's most basic questions. Recite the right formula and you will be saved. We are admonished to declare our utter commitment to certain creedal statements and, as a result, we often become victims of a plaque of certainty. Certainty is not a prize that religion has to offer. Religion is far too eager to turn poetry into prose. In so doing, religions become mere fossils of their origins.

We might ask ourselves: "To what extent has our practice of the Christian religion become a fossil of the Jesus presence?" We should awaken to an understanding that our myths have not only the power to bring hope and solace, they also have the power to maim and destroy. Any religious myth can to be transformed into a destructive force when it claims to know absolute truth absolutely. It happens when our songs of the universe and our poetic lyrics become transformed into religious facts and dogma to be believed. Beware of any religion that has it all figured out.

Myth and ritual, then, are central to our lives, including our lives of faith. Rituals are the enactment of myths. A handshake, for a brief moment, overshadows our separateness. A wedding ceremony sets out the commitment that belongs to the mythology of marriage. In their "twoness," the marriage partners can experience a oneness within. There is a oneness within each of us that we can experience more genuinely in our connectedness to one another. The other person does not make us whole. That is a mistake. It is in being conjoined with another that we experience our own wholeness. The two becoming one enables each of the two to experience his or her own wholeness.

Myth is always central to our religious experience. Yet we have sometimes in our modern, western way tried to obscure myth by trying to turn it into fact. We shall be richer if we never allow ourselves to forgo the power of myth. Descriptive facts, in the words of Ludwig Wittgenstein, tell us "what is the case." Myths lift our spirits and soothe the longings of the heart. We should not confuse myth with fact.

For example, the Garden of Eden is not a place to be discovered on one of our archeological journeys. Now, those journeys are important because they teach us a lot about our human history—about human triumphs and tragedies, many of which we continue to replicate. But the Garden of Eden is not a place out there to be found. Eden is within us. Within that inner garden, there indeed lives today the tree of life and the tree of the knowledge of good and evil. But the human situation is that we live east of Eden. We focus our lives outward. We measure our well-being by the pain and pleasures of our exterior lives.

The redemptive figure in human history and for us as Christians, the Christ-figure, calls us to see again the tree of eternal life within. The experience of salvation is the experience of hearing the eternal within that breaks through the voice of the serpents of conflict and our isolation from one another. We were created to live in the garden, but, like Adam, we become victims of the iconic distractions of our outward lives that hearken us to be our own gods and to take charge of our own destinies. The story of the Garden of Eden is not mostly a story about long ago. It is a myth that has implications for our own present lives. It is the story of how our hyphens of connectivity become walls of separation. Creating myths of God is a wonderfully human thing to do, and myths are the best antidote for absolute religious knowledge. Our lives are enriched by the stories of God, not by the facts about God. We are woefully short on "God facts."

Every enduring world religion begins simply as stories of the divine. These stories are never factual. They might be better described as aesthetic disclosures. The creation stories are not factual stories. The deluge and Noah's Ark are not factual stories. The Exodus is not a factual story. The Virgin Birth is not a factual story. The story of Buddha is not a factual story. For we who call ourselves Christians, our belief is not focused on Jesus as a factual story. One does not become Christian by accepting the fact of Jesus. Jesus was so compelling, not because of the facts he revealed, but because of the stories he told, and a new way of relating that he embodied. The disciples followed him into a new life. Jesus was living a new way of being in the world.

When it comes to speaking of God, the poet and the parable-teller are more powerful and more relevant than the scientist. That is because our being here is a more profound event than the facts about our being here can ever disclose. We are not a collection of inert facts. We are not obituaries. Each one of us is a living, shining star. And I might add that each of us is the brightest ray of light that somebody will ever see.

It sometimes seems difficult to think of our own religion in mythological or metaphorical terms. It is so, in part, because we find it hard to free ourselves of the notion that our faiths are more about the apprehension of facts than the experiencing of the eternal energy of God. Jesus was not bringing the disciples a new set of facts to learn. He brought them a new "God-moment" to experience. When Jesus said, for example, "the truth will set you free," he was clearly not suggesting that the fact of his being there would set them free.

We have to reconsider what we mean by being true. We properly speak of propositions being true or false. But we also speak of true love or discovering our true selves. The true self, which may have religious and theological significance, cannot be offered up as a true proposition.

There are two forms of true propositions. One is a statement for which there is underlying evidence. If a person says, "it is raining," you only need to step outside to confirm the verity of the statement. A second form of truth comes through deductive reasoning. If A = B, and B = C, then for sure, A = C. Deductive propositions are true because they do not tell us anything we didn't know already. They simply draw out what we already knew, but perhaps had not recognized to be true. That can be dangerous, of course, because if you accept a false assumption as true, you can assert anything to be true as a conclusion. Therefore, when someone makes an erroneous assumption, such as the Bible or the Quran is infallible, he can usually conclude all manner of religious nonsense from that false assumption. If we are going to be rationalists, we have to watch our predicates. In brief, propositional truth can be achieved inductively, that is by observation and experimentation, to wit the Hadron Collider, or deductively, discerning new knowledge as an inference from what we already know to be true. Mathematics and logic are the best examples of deductive reasoning. Science and experimentation are best examples of inductive reasoning.

In contrast to these forms of truth, speaking of true love or the true self is an entirely different matter. And that is the kind of truth to which the words of Jesus were referring when he said, "the truth will set you free." When Jesus invited the young fishermen to come with him, he was inviting them to see themselves, perhaps for the first time, in a new light.

When someone says, "I love you," that is not a fact statement. It is a truth statement. (It may not be true, but it is a truth statement.) No amount of inductive evidence will confirm its truth. "I love you" is a relational statement. Its truth cannot be authenticated scientifically or mathematically. So, give up on propositional proof. Love is a risk—always. It bears the risk of hurt, even death. We experience the truth of "I love you" in the actual relationship of loving and being loved. "I love you" is again closer to being an aesthetic disclosure than a fact statement. It is more like saying a compelling work of art is beautiful or a performance of music is moving. The "stirring of the soul" is not a factual observation. It is truth that can only be confirmed experientially and relationally.

Because we conflate truth and fact, religious disillusionment often springs from transforming our myths into menial facts. Religious truth is not based on factual truth. The facts of our religions will not be enough to sustain us. The teachings of our religions are important, but they will not satisfy the longings of the heart.

When we reduce the essence of our lives to the facts of our lives, the facts can become a heavy burden to bear. The facts surrounding our jobs, the facts surrounding our marriages, the facts surrounding our sexuality, the facts surrounding our religious alignments actually never define us. We consistently become so consumed by the daily bread of facts that we cannot hear the inner music that is the sustaining energy of our being.

In Western thought, we have also been hampered by the priority we have placed on subject and object, both in the subject-predicate form of our language and the radical individualism that grew out of the enlightenment. Society is not a collection of discrete individuals; it is a collection of connected individuals, a collection of hyphenated persons.

The failure to recognize that truth accounts for endless crimes and atrocities. Our divisions of human reality into subjects and objects distort what is actually present. For example, we may speak of ourselves as the lover or the loved, a classic subject and object. Friend and enemy might be another. But the lover and the loved or the friend and the enemy exist independently only in a manner of speaking. You are not a discrete object loving another discrete, independent object. You are not a righteous individual killing an unrelated unrighteous enemy. Loving is prior to the lover or the loved. Relating is prior to the righteous or the unrighteous. You are not an isolated subject or an isolated object. You are a derivative of the hyphen. Do not diminish the hyphen. God resides there. As individual selves, we are a derivative of the relationships that give color and texture and character to our lives.

V.

MYTH
THE LANGUAGE OF GOD

The God beyond our gods should not be conceived as a divine object. God is not a separate being up there—wherever "up there" is. God is right here within us and among us. God is in the greening of every spring and the budding of every flower. God is in the setting of every sun and the breaking of every morning. God is in the encouraging call of a friend's voice and the distant look in a stranger's eye. Isaiah heard the angels singing, "the fullness of the earth is God's presence." God is the ultimate creativity that manifests itself in the awesomeness of distant galaxies as well as the awesomeness of a person who is close by. God is pure relationality. God is the togetherness of every coming together. God is the intimacy of connectivity in every experience of authentic human communion. That nothing is entirely separate from anything else turns out to be both a scientific fact and a religious truth.

All of our religious traditions hold in common an effort to account for our lives through metaphor and myth when we have reached the edge of reason. No person lives by reason alone.

Religious doctrines and traditions, whether they be Christian or Buddhist or Hindu or Muslim become crystalized forms of religious experience. Doctrines are the rationalization of faith. Faith opens windows that reason never can. The Buddha means "one who awakens." For the early disciples, Jesus was also an awakening. These young men, later to become disciples, were perhaps perfectly content with their fishing, until they were awakened. They began slowly to see themselves, and to understand their living in ways never before experienced, even though they, like Jesus, had grown up in the midst of a flurry of religious activity. Dutiful religious activity is not a guarantee of experiencing life-changing "God-moments."

If our religious mythologies are to be sustained, they have to be continually recreated out of our own "now" experiences of self-transcendence. Otherwise, we are left to worship words and traditions, which were mythical translations of experiencing God's presence. They were ways of holding on to the "Jesus experience." For the disciples, meeting Jesus was a revolutionary "God-moment" in their lives. Religion often leaves us with only the "dry bones" of faith that have to be brought to life within our own experience.

Jesus seemed to be saying to his followers, "come with me to see the inner light, to listen to your inner music (Kingdom of God within), to sense the person within you that is more than what you see in the mirror, to allow yourself to be reborn into a new way of being in the world." Jesus was hardly urging them to leave their Jewish religion. Jesus was enabling them to experience anew the energy of God's presence within them that had become hidden by the barnacles of their complex exterior lives, including their religious lives.

When we are speaking of the energy of God's presence, we should not imagine that you and I are most likely to go into a closet and meditate long enough to hear God speak out loud. But I do want to say that solitude plays an important role in our lives. Psychologists may call it mindfulness. Rarely does solitude simply mean idleness. There is a time to be idle, to be alone with ourselves without solving any problems or climbing any mountains—to be at rest. But solitude, in contrast to idleness, touches a quiet center within and issues into thoughtful creativity—a change of heart, a work of art, a composition of music, a rendering of poetry, a reflective insight, a righting of injustice. Each such experience, in the moment, may be deeply spiritual or emotional. Solitude enables us to relate more creatively with ourselves and more authentically with someone else. We often see our way more clearly in solitude. I write when I am alone. The poet often conceives verse in the quiet of solitude. Some of the greatest compositions of music spring from solitude. The self-intimacy of solitude enables us to experience ourselves and our world more profoundly. Solitude means that only by becoming present to ourselves can we authentically become present to another person.

For the disciples, meeting Jesus was a transforming and creative event. It should be telling that Jesus did not pursue his life in isolation. After an experience of solitude in the wilderness, he did not withdraw. His entire journey was defined by relating. He called twelve, symbolic of the community of Israel. He taught multitudes on a hillside. He feasted with friends. He wanted his disciples near as he faced dread in an evening of despair.

As Jesus' followers began their own journeys, they naturally wanted to hold on to this experience of Jesus that caught them by surprise. They would never be the same. They wanted to hold on to this transforming way of seeing themselves and their relationships with one another. Their exterior lives of fishing and carpentry could never again completely define them.

The worship of Jesus or, for that matter, the worship of Muhammed or Buddha, is a mistake. It inevitably leads to replacing our existential participation in the universal "Christ" with the addition of religion as one more item on the list of our responsibilities. It is worth noting that the greatest religious seers in human civilization never offered themselves as objects of worship. It is tyrants and demagogues who make such claims.

This proclivity to worship Jesus obscures the power of Jesus' presence. The Last Supper, which has become so central to Christian worship, was not a celebration of the exterior gathering. It was a celebration of interior connectedness. So when we, as Christians, gather around a communion table, we are remembering Jesus, but we are also celebrating the inner connectedness among us because of our common participation in God's presence. Every person around the table, including Judas, is a gift of God to the world. And the world desperately needs us to live out the light within us, a light that has never before been seen and will never reoccur.

The connectedness of our lives never diminishes our individuality. To the contrary, it underscores individuality. No person embodies the relationships that constitute your personal being. No person embodies what you embody. No person can imagine what you can imagine or dream what you can dream. No person can see what you can see or say what you can say or do what you can do or be what you can be. Every person matters because each individual is a gift of light to the world.

While the historical Jesus may be very important to those of us who call ourselves Christian, the story of Jesus as a new kind of presence is far more important. I do not believe that we have to find the historical bones of Jesus to see the light that Jesus revealed. Jesus surely was not trying to set up a new world religion. That observation is not to say that the birthing of Christianity was a bad consequence. Christianity has been a great source of healing and hope and, like other world faiths, has sometimes been used for evil and destructive purposes. But birthing a new religion did not appear to be the compelling priority of Jesus' life. Tearing people away from their Jewish worship did not seem to be his ambition. He was calling people to experience God's presence within the immediacy of their own being here. Jesus wanted people to see themselves in a new light. Worshiping Jesus is not the defining content of Christianity. Being in the world in a new way, seeing that new light that informs our self-understanding as well as our understanding of others and the world is the defining content of religious experience. Being a Christian or a Buddhist or a Jew is about an existential participation in the "way" that transforms our lives.

Religious practice and thought sometimes blocks the light of God's presence. The Christian faith should not be defined as believing in Jesus.

There are a lot more people willing to believe in Jesus and to confess allegiance to Jesus than are willing actually to follow him. For Christians, the Jesus event, if it becomes a centering force in their lives, turns on a new light, a new way of seeing. Following Jesus enables Christians to see the contours of their lives in a new dimension and to see others and their world very differently.

Christians, of course, need to remind themselves that the stories and the myths and the parables that give them new light are not the only holy stories that can enlighten and inspire us. The birth of religion is the story of human transcendence. It may have begun as primitive art on the walls of caves among the earliest homo sapiens. Those drawings on a cave wall told a story. A common thread among all our religions is that each has a story. Every religion and every person's life forms a mythology. Your story frames your self-understanding and the meaning of your being here. That is why biographies are so appealing. We want to read the story of another—to see within them. If we have the heart to listen, the stories of others can enlighten us. They can inspire us. They can enrich our own stories.

In contrast to myth, science tends to be linear in its growing understanding of the world. Their discoveries pose new questions, from which follow new discoveries and new questions. The works of art and music and religion are more episodic than linear. Writers and artists and musicians and prophets are continually casting a new eye. They are reinterpreting the world. Whereas the scientist aims toward the acquisition of factual knowledge, the poet and the prophet aims toward new insight. Poets and prophets engage in an aesthetic interplay with the world. Of course the seeing of a poet or a prophet cannot be verified or confirmed by external experiments. The scientist enables us to know; the artist enables us to see.

We should want all the knowledge that science can provide. But knowledge alone turns out to be insufficient fuel for our human journeys. We do not live by knowledge alone. Experiencing the creative forces alive within us enables us to become more fully human, more fully alive to our own interconnected being.

When we genuinely experience our interrelatedness, we are touching the meaning of eternity. The Eternal is not a reference to something out yonder in a narrative of the future. The eternal lies within each of us here and now. All that ever was or will be lies within us. Science tells us in the language of equations, and religion tells us in the language of myth that our creative essence has no end. Every person is an embodiment of the eternal.

We are the incarnations of God's presence. We are not replicas of a god who resides in a remote place among the stars. In the metaphor of Buddhism, every person embodies the Buddha waiting to be awakened as one renounces the clutches of exterior preoccupations. Only your exterior self, your self as an isolated subject, wants you to belong to a certain religion, to be an orthodox Jew, or a Methodist Christian, or a Sunni Muslim, or a Mayahana Buddhist. At their highest, our faith stories are recollections of experiencing the Eternal. Worship creates new faith stories. Jesus would likely not recognize Christianity today. Too few persons have the courage actually to enter into the Jesus story. Muhammed would surely weep over the abuses of Islam. The Muhammed story is being lost and destroyed in every episode of brutality and wanton destruction.

All our talk of God staggers under the weight of bundles of religious affirmations that are asserted to be true and that we are expected to believe. This dilemma especially seems to plague Christianity, Islam, and Judaism more than Eastern religions. No set of religious doctrines will ever show us the way to the Eternal. Neither doctrines nor creeds should be denigrated, but the teaching of doctrine and the recitation of creeds must be linked to experiences of holiness that often elude description except in the form of story or myth or metaphor. Myth, not doctrine, is the language of God. Teaching and recitation need to be connected with experiencing the godness that lives within each of us, or like the disciples, experiencing the "God-moment" in their encounter with Jesus.

Story and parable, poetry and music, the modalities of mythologies, are deeply revealing resources that should not be shunted aside. We are not going to find God in our explorations of space. Heaven does not exist out there as an outpost amidst the galaxies. We may have to let go of the fact of God, if we are to experience the truth of God. Of the truth of God, we can either be silent or we can sing. We can be silent or we can kneel. We can be silent or we can shout. Music and art and myth are the languages that ignite the power of the ultimate and transcendent oneness that lives within every soul.

Let us be inspired, by which I mean, "inspirited" by the inward and mythical journey of others. The idea that God prefers one religion over another is nothing more than self-indulgent narcissism. God resides in the yearning heart of every person. I am confident the voice of God lies behind many religious initiatives. Yet, in saying that God does not prefer a particular religion, I am not suggesting that all religions are created equal. We should confess that our history of religions is filled with a mixture of good and evil, of insight and blindness. Some religions, even some churches or synagogues or mosques or temples, become greater sources of enlightenment than others. The issue is whether the stories and teachings and myths of our faiths enlighten and inspire followers to engage the godness within their own lives, as well as the sanctity of one another and the sacredness of the world in which we live.

The affirmation of our faiths as well as the behavior and beliefs that they foster do matter. Our human myths are subject to being exploited and abused. That exploitation and abuse often yields tragedy. The stories of the Quran, and the Jewish Torah, and the Christian Old Testament can be used as justifications for murderous actions. In fact, the stories of the New Testament were used to justify the injustices of slavery and segregation. They are now being used to justify injustice towards lesbians and gays and bisexuals and transgender individuals. The stories of Muhammed can and are being used to justify brutality and violence. Hindu stories have sometimes been hijacked to justify atrocities. Our human stories can become twisted into evil parodies.

So the stories of our faiths and the experiences that generate our myths have to be continually rewritten. We cannot live off yesterday's stories. Reciting yesterday's stories will not be enough. Our life scripts have to be written anew. The myth of Jesus must be born again in the immediacy of our own experience. The immediacy of creating a more just and peaceful world must supplant our outworn myths of privilege and prejudice. The light must turn on in my own life and in our own society. Jesus must become a living experience. Similarly, the goal of Buddhism is not the worship of Buddha. The goal of Buddhism is to become the Buddha—to become one who is awakened by the ecstasy of encountering the Kingdom of God within. That is the nearest place God has a Kingdom.

Instead of worshipping yesterday's stories, those stories should ignite within us the passion for writing new stories of the light of the Eternal breaking in upon us. New light changes everything. It changes how we see ourselves. It changes how we see others. It changes how we see our presence in the universe.

The triumph of our myths of God is not to gain a grip on God. The triumph is to be set free to live our interdependent lives more authentically. Our images of the Eternal become our mythical masks of God. Every acorn, every galaxy, every exoplanet, every earth 2.0 is the presence of God in disguise. Hold it high. Treasure its power. Myth is the language of the soul.

VI.

ENGAGING MYSTERY WITH IMAGINATION

You and I live in an awesome, but mysterious world. So far, we have learned that we live in a world in which the things we see with our eyes are often not what they appear. Our language seems only a rough approximation of what we experience. Therefore, how do we deal with this world in which the reality of things may be radically different than how they may appear? Whether a scientist or a person of faith, traversing the mystery requires imagination.

In high school physics and chemistry, we learned that tables and chairs, not to speak of persons or stars, are made of atoms and molecules. In fact, there is an entire zoo of particles more elementary than either atoms or molecules. They include electrons and protons and neutrons, and protons themselves are made up of such weird-sounding things as quarks and gluons. To be even more basic, everything out there and in here, everything in your reading room, including you, as well as our chairs and lecterns, is made up of two fundamental kinds of particles. Scientists call those particles bosons and fermions. (If you think the mythology of religion is remarkable, recognize that science has built a mythology of its own.) Bosons are particles that carry the forces that impinge upon us, all of us, every day. They include the electromagnetic force, the force of gravity, and the strong and weak nuclear forces within atoms. Fermions are matter particles out of which our tables and chairs are made. The particles themselves are simply fluctuations or vibrations within the fabric of the universe and all of them are interrelated. There are no unrelated particles.

Now, most important of all, as we observe this incredibly mysterious world, is that everything, every particle, every star, every person, is simply a form of energy. That is what $E = mc^2$ means. That simple equation was the most important equation of the 20th century. That equation not only changed science. It changed the entire geo-political world. This one formula was the foundation of the nuclear revolution. $E = mc^2$ may not be a rule that governs other universes, but it seems to be a basic rule that governs our universe.

This rule of our universe tells us, among other things, that you and I and everything around us are constellations of related energy, congealed into matter. Let me repeat a critical truth: matter and energy are essentially one. They are different forms of the interrelatedness of all existence. That means, of course, that the material and the spiritual are the same thing. There is not a material world alongside a spiritual world. The material world is simply one face of the spiritual world. There is not a divine world alongside a secular world. There is only one world and it may be far greater than our vast universe. The world is more mysterious than we ever dreamed.

When it comes to understanding our world, you and I clearly have a bias toward the material. That bias is certainly not surprising since our dominant experience takes place within the world of matter. Matter is our playground. Scientists are helping us learn (and our learning can be instructive for faith) that those things toward which we have such a strong bias may be among the least basic things in the world. It may be unsettling. In this weird world, however, we have learned that objects and entities are no longer the prime real estate for understanding what's going on in our world.

The chairs on which are sitting and the lectern from which I might be speaking, the white board on which I might be writing, are not solid substantive things after all. Well, they certainly feel solid. We can put our weight down on them. In reality, however, they are not really solid at all. The lectern is mostly made up of empty space. The chair on which you are sitting is mostly empty space.

These are not actually as solid as they appear. They are a vibrating mass of particles.

Your chair, like a bolt of lightning, is made of electrically charged particles and the forces among those particles. These forces and these particles are teeming with activity. What appears to be still is actually moving very rapidly. This activity is not random. It is governed by laws, and the equilibrium of those interrelated forces and activities are keeping your chair in place. If one of those forces disappeared, say gravity, your chair would float away. Without gravity, all of our chairs would have to be nailed down. But of course, the boards to which you nailed them wouldn't stay in place either. A strange world.

This mysterious world is one in which relatedness prevails, not things. It is a world in which matter, all of it, everything you see or touch, is simply a slow version of energy. It is captured energy.

Things, then, are sometimes not what they appear. For example, we cannot see most of the light in the world. We cannot see the longer wave lengths of light, such as microwaves or radio waves. We cannot see the shorter wave lengths of light, such as x-rays or gamma rays. We can see the middle range of wave lengths, which is visible light. So, solid things are not solid, most light is hidden from our eyes, and our time calculations are completely relative. Mystery is abundant.

Some of you may remember the famous twin paradox first described by Albert Einstein, but later verified by scientific measurements. The twin paradox goes like this: Let's suppose that twins are born. One stays here on earth. The other is placed in our hypothetical spaceship leaving earth at speeds approaching the speed of light. Let's suppose the spaceship is traveling at 90% of the speed of light. This twin's clock will be moving at 44% of the speed of his brother's clock on earth. And not just his clock. The spaceship and everything in his world will be aging at that slower rate. Time will slow down.

Let's increase the speed from 90% to 99%. The boy's clock, as well as his world will age at 14% of his brother on earth. Let's ratchet the speed on up to 99.9% of the speed of light. At that speed, his time is moving at 4.5% of his brother's time on Earth. So, if the rocket ship is going 99.9% of the speed of light, and five years later he comes back to earth, he will obviously be five years old. However, his brother, who remained on earth, whose clock has been moving much faster, will be 110 years. Time is not what it seems. We do not live in time. Time lives in us. We do indeed live in a mysterious world.

Our bias toward material things diminishes our perception of non-material things. For example, energy. You cannot put a handful of energy in your pocket and then later retrieve it. There is energy all about us here, in your pocket as well as within us. We are swimming in it, whether sitting or standing, wherever we are. However, because we cannot see it or get a handful of that energy, it may seem less real.

Our stubborn bias also diminishes perceived realities such as hope or joy, not to speak of peace or love. Those are not hard, substantial things that you can pick up and put on a shelf. Because they cannot be corralled, we are inclined to deem them to be less real. We might say those are just feelings. Or, those are simply states of mind. In reality, hope is a configuration of energy as surely as is a rock. Joy is a configuration of energy as surely as the chair on which you are sitting. Love is a configuration of energy as surely as is our physical body. Whether we are speaking of rocks or hope, we are speaking of constellations of relatedness. We are talking about ways of being in the world.

Our old views of ourselves and even some of our views of God may not work in this mysterious but awesome world in which we live. It is time to reform our thinking. Perhaps our ideas about God also need to be rethought. Our ideas and our encounters with other people are certainly not what they may seem and that should change how we behave. People are not objects completely outside us. We are profoundly interconnected and interdependent upon one another. Every person who exists, every person who ever existed is brother or sister to us. The call and the compelling need for respect is built into the human situation. God, too, is not a thing in the world, completely outside us. God is both beyond and within us, and our lives are deeply intertwined with both the beyond and the within. We may choose to ignore it, but we are all bound to the sacred.

You may want to speak of energy as spirit. That's ok. Spirit works. Relatedness works. Thingness doesn't. You cannot put a handful of spirit in your pocket, but you can put it on a canvas. You can compose inspiring music. You can put spirit into meeting someone person to person and heart to heart. Rocks are sandy and unstable. They belong to a secondary order of reality. Secondary does not suggest that it is unimportant. It is as important as the stars above. But it is not primary. The energy reality, the spirit reality belongs to the first and primary order. That which seems mysterious because we cannot grasp it with our hands or see it with our eyes or comprehend it with our minds may be the most enduring of all. Our sun, which warms our days, has a life cycle of about 10 billion years. We are about half way through that cycle. So while it will last a long time, it is not reliable as an enduring object. Our sun will burn out.

God-talk in a "big bang" world should be shaped around a new way of seeing our world. Developing new ways of thinking and talking about God can lead us to a new way of understanding our being here. We can learn to hear the voice and understand the presence of the sacred within us.

Throughout these essays, I have been affirming three things, the first two of which I have mostly discussed earlier: Here, I will focus mostly on the third, the nature and reality of God.

1. Things are not things. They are not enduring and hard substances. They are events born of a constellation of connectivity. At best, they are expressions of a more enduring reality. Things are episodic vibrations in the field of being.

2. People are not objects that you can put into a place. They are episodes of light and interrelatedness. We are all interdependent. Vicious wars, genocide, malicious killings wither the human soul. When we hurt another person, the pain reverberates within us. That is a universal truth built into our essence.

3. God does not exist as a being in the world. The reality of God is the divine energy that we ex-

perience as sacred mystery and that courses throughout our world and perhaps countless other universes as well.

That famous formula, $E = mc^2$ was the scientific afterthought of trying to understand this diversity of energy and matter. In religion, God is the afterthought of coping with the mystery of Eternity—the reality out of which time was born.

We should not allow the transcendence or the "godness" of mystery to escape us. Mystery means otherness. There is an otherness to the mystery that remains beyond our grasp. The transcendence of mystery is apparent in science and foundational for faith. In every case, scientific inquiry, including our listening to the echoes of cosmic radiation that has led scientists to postulate the "big bang," drives us back to what scientists have called "planck time," a time which denotes the horizons of time itself. It takes us back to utter transcendent mystery, which leaves every scientist in silence because we have no words to describe it. We should think of "planck time" as a mythological term, not a descriptive term.

People of faith, as different as Christian and Hindu, speak of the transcendent mystery as God. We are awed both by its otherness as well as its intimate embrace. God is a name we give to the ineffable, the unintelligible, the utter otherness of mystery in which we are immersed, because standing within the transcendent mystery in silence is more than we can bear. We must shout "God." It is not so much that we actually have identified a transcendent God. Rather in our religious language, transcendence is what we are alluding to in all our myths of God.

The transcendent mystery eludes our capture in existence or language. God-talk soothes our souls as we are confronted with the unspeakable transcendence that is beyond language or knowing. Transcendence does not suffer the chains of our temporal and spiritual lives and our experience of transcendence lies not in knowing or speaking, but in being. Each of us is transcendence taking on flesh and living in space and time in our vast universe, and, though vast, our universe may be only one among an infinite number of the manifestations of universal transcendence.

In our God-talk, we name our gods—whether Yahweh or Allah or, in Eastern traditions, the Way or the Brahman. It is our infant-like effort to demystify our being here, to bring utter otherness down to earth.

We need a personal God, in part, because we are persons. We need to know that there is a "person"—a mother, a father—that cares for us. We become compelled to create God in our own image. That need seems intrinsic to our human situation.

Our images enable us to relate to God's presence in a more personal and emotional way. I think that we should never decry our personal images of God. Our experiences of God are highly personal, whether speaking of Jesus or a friend who was beside you when your life was hurting. The challenge is not to translate personal into being a lone object out there. Neither God nor your friend is a lone object out there. They belong to your inner being. The transcendent otherness is not mostly out there in the mighty and raging storms. It is also down deep within, beckoning us to be still.

The more you come to know yourself, through science or religion or psychology, the more you begin to discern your essential relatedness to all beings. Every other person is also a transcendent being to whom we are related. Both science and religion are leading us there. Another's pain really is, in part, our own. The mourning of the loss of family or friend comes from the real loss of a part of our own being. The isolated individual, as I have previously underscored, is pure pretense. We can know ourselves profoundly and we can experience God's presence only when our human journey enables us to connect more authentically, more emotionally, more inclusively. I believe that our human interactions are the reservoir of our deepest spiritual experiences.

We human beings may not be the highest form of life in the universe. But we can see the world only from where we stand, and we acknowledge that, after all, we may not be alone. In our remote corner of this mysterious world, we are cultivating human intelligence, which during this century will make extraordinary leaps. We are conjoining the thinking machine with the human brain. We are exponentially increasing the power of the human mind. Because we have deciphered the genetic code, natural selection evolution is being augmented by volitional evolution. We can create our own mutations. We can clone human parts and perhaps even new persons. Frankly, doing so can spell progress or demise. We now have the capacity to change human destiny. But are we wise enough? Our hope is that the convergence of mind and machine and the augmenting of natural selection with volitional evolution, though fraught with enormous ethical dilemmas, will help us understand and improve the human condition. But, we are uncertain.

Living in an uncertain world should teach us that living well in our world will not only require intelligence; it will indeed require imagination. I cite one observation from Albert Einstein that I think may be his most insightful reflection. He said, "Imagination is more important than knowledge." Imagination is good for the mind and the soul. It should not be confused with flights of fantasy or daydreaming. Fantasy is the absence of being present with yourself. Imagination begins with thoughtful reflection, practicing becoming at home with yourself. The advances of Copernicus or Galileo or Sir Isaac Newton would have never been achieved without imagination. We would never have had the general or the special theory of relativity without imagination. The courage of the Pakistani young woman, Malala, would never have arisen without her imagination. We would never have traveled to the moon without imagination. We will never overcome wars without imagination. We will not overcome warring religions without imagination. The interiority of imagination enables us to escape the biases of our exterior lives.

I am also confident that we cannot reshape our understanding of God without imagination. Intelligence will not be enough. Doctrines will not be enough. More religious institutions will not be enough. Faith requires imagination. In this world in which our seeing is so limited, imagination may be required to see the Eternal Light, by which I mean the light that lies outside time but that enlightens our lives. Our intelligence will not lead us to grasp God. Living with the compelling mystery and reaching toward the Godness beyond our gods requires that we embrace the power of imagination.

VII.

LOVE
A METAPHOR FOR OUR
ULTIMATE RELATEDNESS

I am a thoroughgoing universalist. I believe that you and I, all of us, are episodes of God's presence. It is not so much that we know God; God knows us. We do not possess God. God possesses us. It is not that we have a hold on God. God has a hold on us. Each person is a gift of God's light to the world. When each of us is born, God says, "Let there be light."

Every act of public worship, every moment of solitude, and, especially, every act of relating, person to person, heart to heart, is an experience of the sanctity of our being here. You and I have seen and known people who have the imagination to align their lives more fully with the godness of the universe. They are not all Christians, of course. I think of Mahatma Gandhi who said, "I would have been a Christian had it not been for Christians." We might think of Mother Teresa or Pope Francis. The gift of Mother Teresa or Pope Francis is not in their rationality. It is in their relationality. The power of Pope Francis is not his talking about the poor; it is his touching the poor. It is not about his homilies regarding the prisoners and the downtrodden; it is about his embracing them in flesh. Francis and Teresa were and are not so much people of great reason; they were and are people of great relating.

Apart from the famous and well known, there are those in our own personal worlds who embody this higher alignment. We usually call them saints. A person is not a saint because he or she believes the right things. Frederick Buechner described saints as "life-givers." Sainthood is more about the person you become by experiencing a greater alignment that comes through seeing that your wellbeing is interwoven with the wellbeing of others.

The over-objectification of our lives is a pernicious problem that obscures the connectedness of our lives. You and I are activities of God in the world. Adam was an activity of God and so are we. We should claim that reality. We should embrace its power. We are prone to lose our way in our Adam-like living that divorces ourselves from the Eternal within which we live. We, like Adam, prefer to stand on our own. It is a fool's game. We always fail. Sacred relatedness is our reality. In our rush to see everyone and everything else as things external to us, holding others at arm's length, we lose all touch with the essential reality that we are one. Nothing is external to us.

In our mysterious world, I believe Jesus was on to something, and, frankly, I think it was the same something that Abraham and the Buddha and Confucius came to experience.

The Torah is purported to have 613 laws. In that context, we remember that someone approached Jesus to ask what was the law that mattered most. Because there are many of them and Jesus was a faithful Jew, Jesus could have said, of course, "They all matter." Instead, Jesus said, "Love God with all that is within you and love other people as you love yourself." Let's get this. Love is the metaphor Jesus chose to underscore as the sacred way of relating. Jesus said that loving, perhaps the highest form of relating that we can put into language, is what matters most. If we could use our imagination to rescue the word and regain its energy, perhaps loving could become a clue to what our inner godness looks like in flesh and blood.

Frankly, rescuing that word is a tall order, because we have too often converted love into a theological doctrine or an ephemeral feeling. One of the great challenges to understanding loving as an expression of God's presence is that we live largely in a binary world:

> Love and hate
> Light and darkness

Good and evil
Yin and Yang
Sacred and profane
Masculine and feminine.

With all of these bifurcations, can we ever get in touch with the oneness from which these antitheses sprang? I remind you, the bifurcations exist only in time. The mythical Eden was innocent of opposites. East of Eden, they lived in a world of opposites—Adam and Eve, Cain and Abel, Moses and Pharaoh, Jesus and Mary Magdalene.

In our post-Eden, binary world, we are left to struggle with such dualisms as masculine and feminine, good and evil, peace and war. Relating transcends opposites. Loving brings wholeness to a world that is splintered by living "over against" one another. Let's explore, for example, the opposites of masculine and feminine and how that dualism has shaped and, in some cases, crippled our spiritual understanding.

In reality, the masculine and the feminine resides in each of us. Yet in the Christian faith (and I believe it is true for Judaism and Islam), our notions of God have been dominated by the masculine. God is male. God is power. God is control. God is Lawgiver. Western thought, generally, sets forth a masculine god.

As a religious culture, we Western Christians have been far less in touch with the feminine side of God. God is nurturer. God is caregiver. God is servant. God is the womb in which the universe resides. If rationality is considered the masculine side of God, relatedness would be the feminine side of God.

The myth of the Virgin Birth, for example, emphasizes the feminine dimension of Jesus' presence. Without male intervention, Mary conceives and bears a son. Mary, the mother of God. The Son of Man was an issue of feminine reality. The prominence of Mary Magdalene also underscores the feminine Jesus. It was Mary Magdalene who first saw that love does not stay buried. Neither light nor love are subject to death.

In reality, of course, God is transgender. We are inclined to rationalize our experience of God to make it conform to our dualistic world of masculine and feminine. Science explores the masculine manifestation of the ultimate singularity. Science prefers reason. Faith's role is not to put down the rationality of science, but to keep us in touch with the relationality of faith. Yet, in fact, in our Western traditions, the masculine has prevailed both in science and religion.

Masculine authority has been the hallmark of our religion—the authority of Scripture, the authority of the Church, the authority of creeds, the authority of the Priest or the Preacher. Perhaps it will be a sign that we are recovering from a masculine-dominated religion when a woman is elected as Pope. You say that will take a 1,000 years, but remember the "Nowness" of the Eternal. A thousand years is but a "day." (As an aside, the distinction between Pope Benedict and Pope Francis is that Benedict appeared more thoroughly masculine, rational, and firmly authoritative. To the consternation of the male-dominated Curia, Francis appears masculine in his approach to the Curia and the machinations of the Church hierarchy, but as pastor and priest he appears feminine).

If we are to understand Jesus' words regarding love, I believe we will have to recover the feminine dimension of God, the wisdom of God, the suffering God, the embracing, unencumbered lovingness of God, the womb-likeness of God. I am appealing here to the energy of God, not the thingness of God.

We simply cannot make sense of the relatedness of our being without including the feminine. The masculine too often seems intent on turning love into a doctrine to be believed. We are too eager to construe love as a truth to be affirmed, a word to be spoken. Love is not a commandment (authority and power) to be agreed to or to recite. Love is a powerful metaphor pointing toward the purest form of relatedness. Jesus and Mary Magdalene together are the full word incarnate.

Christianity, Islam, and Judaism are all very masculine religions. Is this also why they are the world's most violent religions? Peace and suffering, lifting up the meek, accepting the outcasts, caring for the poor, embracing the broken, healing the hurt are thoroughly feminine. I have been inclined to say that men are rational. Women are wise. The masculine makes war. The feminine makes peace. I believe that we will never be able to foster grace and peace and unwarranted forgiveness until we integrate within our understanding and our living the feminine side of God. The calling of God is not only to think; our calling is also to relate.

The mystery of our common life that transcends our dualities runs deep within us. In the final analysis, if we want to experience the deepest creative energy that runs through us and every other person, we have to embrace the risk of loving without condition. It requires thinking and relating. We do not need to believe in love. We do not need to advocate love. We simply have to embrace the other person as an integral part of our own being. So, loving is not language. We need to reach for a more robust understanding of love. For example, love without justice is a broken metaphor. Loving is not a theological doctrine. Loving is a way of being in the world. Loving is a way of being fully present to another person. It is a way of affirming both the maleness and the femaleness of our being here. Rationality without relationality is empty and misses the mark of both understanding God and understanding the essence of our own lives.

Love is an uncommon experience. At our best, we live lives of quiet affection. Affection is a good and joyous thing. Deep and genuine affection is a profoundly creative experience—an experience in which we let go sufficiently of self-interest that we warmly embrace the significance of another person to our own personal lives. Jesus himself mostly lived a life of deep affection for his disciples, for his mother, Mary, and for Mary Magdalene who seemed to be his soul partner.

Love is not simply a state of relating. It is an event in relating. It happened at the well as Jesus met the adulterous woman. It happened at the sycamore tree when Jesus called down the tax collector. It happened on the cross when Jesus said, "Father forgive them for they know not what they are doing."

This kind of love is not subject to human explanation. It is transcendent love. Love cannot be explained by reason alone. Love lies beyond reason. Love comes into the terrain of our interconnectedness lives like new light. Love is that transcendent grace that asks forgiveness for a killer. Reason alone does not prompt us to reach out to those who have been socially cast aside. That is not a rational act; it is an act of faith. There is an otherness, a non-rationality to love that belongs to the nature of mystery. Love, when it happens, cannot be explained. It can only be experienced. The experience of loving and being loved is more than can be annotated by the canons of reason. Affection can be annotated. It can be described. The act of loving is a transcendent, redemptive fire that can only be inferred from the residue of the experience of loving and being loved.

In truth, love rarely happens to us. When it does we are never quite the same. It changes everything. Love is known by faith more than it is known as a rational conclusion. Living in the light and hope of redemptive love is ultimately an act of faith. We are mostly, however, people of little faith. Like Adam, we prefer the assurance of taking charge and the assurance of mutual affection. Affection is an aesthetic experience. Love is an ontological experience. It is the experience of communing with the utter otherness of others and experiencing the mystery of God's presence.

Science teaches us to become more mindful of the elements of creation. Religion teaches us to listen to the sounds of transcendence. The energy that comes from an awareness of transcendence can transform us from being merely sentient beings to becoming aware of our participation in eternal being. The tools of science are reason and observation. The tools of religion are reason and faith.

The energy of transcendence is not the energy of $E = mc^2$. The energy of our universe, under certain circumstances, takes on the face of matter—our natural world. Every tree, and every star and every person is a collection of energy captured in matter and flesh. But the transcendent energy of the universe, shrouded with mystery and largely inexplicable, is surely present in our world. In human terms, I believe that the transcendent energy within the creation of our universe and perhaps countless multiverses is experienced by mere mortals as ultimate love that, from time to time, breaks into our order. I believe that love is the eternal energy of the universe manifested in human flesh. That transcendent love is not to be captured finally within anyone's religion. Nevertheless, it is not at all surprising that when the light breaks, it often spawns efforts to record it and preserve that light. The recollections of the breaking of light later becomes crystalized in our religious forms.

Love, then, I believe, is the energy of God. I have come to the view that the consummate metaphor for speaking for the "un-noun-like" transcendent mystery is the Eternal Now. In our human experience, that Eternal Now comes into our lives as Love. Love is the ultimate language of the human soul that lives out God's Eternal Presence. All of creation, all of the 13.8 billion years of our creation event is, poetically, only a "day" in the being of God. God is the enduring *Now*. God does not exist in time. All that is or ever will be exists in the loving "Nowness" of God. You and I, as well, are events in an ultimate "God-moment."

All our histories and all our futures have reality only in the immediacy of God's presence. When we think about our being here, we are only actually here in the immediacy of God's Now-moment. The present does not exist as a moment in time; it exists as a moment in eternity. In the present, in the Now-moment, we are one with God. Time is only an abstraction. It is a form of measurement. The reality of the past is its presence in the present as memory or regret. While we may be dragged down by the past or fear the future, we can live, truly live, only in the present. The present is the holy moment between the "no longer" and the "not yet" of our lives. That's where we create our being here—in that present moment between the "not yet" and the "no longer."

Past and future are, after all, simply human constructs. They do not exist in eternity. Eternity represents the fulfillment of the past and the future, because, in the Eternal Now, everything is present. The "Now" of our lives is not a moment in time; it is a moment in eternity.

I think of each of us as a flash of light. We like to measure our existence. In time, we may live 45 years or 95 years. Whether 45 or 95 or 105, each of us is God's consummate creation of light. That flash of light that bears your name will never un-flash. It is eternal.

We are far too time–centric in our self-understanding. Time is a poor yardstick to use in accounting for our lives. The measuring of our lives by the clock leads inevitably to a dead end. Our clock will stop. The whole point of faith is to teach us to measure our lives by the only reality we actual-ly experience—the Now-Moment in which eternity is actually present in our presence. The holiest mo-ment in your life is Now. Embrace it. You are a gift that has never before happened in the universe. The whole cosmos converges into your light-bearing presence.

In the immediacy of the present, faith is believ-ing. Faith is doubting. Faith is carrying a cup of wa-ter. Faith is listening to somebody's pain. Faith is wrapping somebody's wounds. Faith is righting yesterday's wrong. Faith is holding somebody who is trembling with fear. Faith is forgiving somebody who "cut you to the quick." Faith is accepting someone who is unacceptable. Faith is lifting up somebody who put you down. Faith is allowing the Eternal Presence to live in your present moment. Believing, doubting, carrying, wrapping, righting, holding, listening, forgiving, accepting, lifting up in the immediate experience of our lives, is the essence of religious faith.

Love travels at the speed of light. I believe that love is the ultimate energy of the universe. It is not a word; it is an act, the energy of believing and doubting. It is the energy of wrapping wounds, of listening to a broken heart. It is the energy of righting wrongs and lifting up those who have been put down. I believe that love is our best human metaphor for the ultimate energy of the universe. Loving is our living out the ultimate relationality of God's presence within us.

In our experience, we know that love is not bound by spatial or temporal categories. The energy of love transcends time and place. Love is Now or it is not at all. We cannot love somebody in the past. We cannot love somebody in the future. Now is the ultimate reality of love. Love is the energy of God captured in human relatedness.

We have learned that all matter decays. Atoms decay. We should not stake our life on them. The transcendent energy of God is eternal. Our physical bodies are here and gone in a whisper. Far beyond physical presence, your life is poetry never before composed. Live your poetry. Poetry is not bound by time. You are living light. Let it breach the darkness. Your personality is pure energy. Your character is pure energy. Your hope is pure light. Your loving is eternal light, a light that never burns out. Your being here is a gift of light.

If we are to speak of the reality of love, we should also face up to the problems of evil. We have to speak of a world where love seems not to be present. We should speak of it in at least two dimensions. First, I speak of suffering and pain and the unexpected tragedies that strike at the heart of every person. Tectonic plates shift. Human cells mutate. Viruses emerge into our lives from the underbrush. There are still too many who wish to explain and, in some cases, justify these experiences of suffering by ascribing that suffering to a harsh or punishing god out there. The truth is closer to where we live. We do not live in a perfect world. We live in a world that is still in the throes of creation. We live in a world where chaos frequently erupts. Our world order lies somewhere between chaos and order. And while chaos happens and rips us apart, that chaos can never override the reality of one's creative presence. God is at work creating the world through you and me. Our world is not yet perfected. Its imperfections, which includes our own twisted mindsets and poor judgments, erupts in troubled lives and broken promises. To this form of suffering, the author of *The Best Exotic Marigold Hotel* made a prescient and theologically relevant remark. He said, "In the end, everything will be all right; if it is not all right, it is not yet the end." Order will prevail. Suffering is never life's final word.

The second dimension of evil is even more troubling. Evil arises because some people are responsible for horrific and unconscionable acts. People commit violent crimes and unthinkable atrocities and even genocide. The holocaust showed the depth of the human capacity for evil. Some stars flame out. If every person is a packet of light in the world, it is possible for one's light to go dark. We should also recognize that it is possible to burn out from the accumulated negativity of leading petty and petulant lives. It is an emptiness into which we can descend slowly every day by thoughtlessness, harshness, putting people down, and a perpetual disdain for human imperfections that infest us all. A petty arrogance seeks to mask our own failures and inadequacies by diminishing other people. We can sink into a hell of our own making. Insofar as we deny or destroy the essential relatedness that binds us one to another, we are, metaphorically speaking, snuffing out our light. We are falling into a virtual "black hole" of human existence. The power of one's incarnation of holiness may be lost in time. However, I believe that the light that made each one's presence possible is redeemed in eternity.

No light is ever lost. I am suggesting here that some stars burn out and so do some humans. Burning out is a temporal episode. Burning out does not mean the loss of the creative energy that creates life. It requires courage and imagination to embrace the reality that the ashes of defeat and evil will be transformed into light. Behaving and living as though that is true is the ultimate act of faith. I believe that every life will be redeemed. The light of the Eternal is never lost. I believe that every burst of light is fully reclaimed within the infinite sea of God's being.

Evil is existentially real and devastating in its impact, but evil and tragedy are never the final word. Evil is not an ontological reality. Evil is not a metaphysical reality. There is no hell except the ones we create. We should not define our lives or define human history by the episodes of darkness, but by the stars that light the night. Eternity will prevail.

If we are to speak fairly and comprehensively about the problem of chaos and disorder in the world, we should acknowledge the Second Law of Thermodynamics, also commonly known as "Entropy." This law indicates that time moves from order to disorder. So, we might account for evil or chaos as the irreversible slide of entropy. Sandcastles disintegrate. Trees fall in the forest and decay. Life withers and dies. Entropy is evident throughout the created world. Entropy is inexorable. But while being a physical law that governs our world with which we must reckon, we should not presume to impose this description of our time-laden, created world to be the final or ultimate word of this or other universes.

Every disorder becomes a platform for creativity. The "big bang" itself presumably occurred in the context of infinitely dense teeming chaotic energy out of which our universe emerged as a creative episode from which space and time as well as far-flung galaxies are being created. Entropy, then, belongs to the vicissitudes of creation, but creativity is the ultimate corollary to entropy. It is important to underscore that entropy is an inexorable law that seems to define and to establish the course of our time-bound world. Like evil, however, entropy is a temporal fact, but not an eternal truth. Entropy is a scientific description of the inevitable outcome of our created world. Suns burn out. Galaxies collide. Our houses collapse. People die. Creativity means, and in theological language, redemption means that collapse and disarray and even death are not the end of the story.

On a human level, disorder and uncertainty have to be met with imagination. Imagination is the fuel of creativity. For all of us, brokenness happens, but we are all broken in different places. The uncertainty that is bred by brokenness can lead us toward utter paralysis. It is the paralysis of entropy. Our greatest resource for dealing with our brokenness always turns out to be the power of imagination. Imagination conceives a new song. Imagination plants a new tree. Imagination builds a new sandcastle. It is imagination that enables us to see and to live beyond where we have been and not to become trapped by the uncertainty and the hurt of temporal defeat. Imagination is what inspired a disillusioned and broken cadre of traumatized disciples to see the transforming wonder of a resurrected life and to become the voices of light and hope for generations to come.

Circling back to the beginning, we have learned that the particle, dubbed the Higgs boson, is not a particle at all. It is a pervasive field through which and in which all particles occur. Imagine God beyond our gods, then, not as a being out there, but as the ultimate field of being, a field of pure interconnectedness, that gives reality and hope and promise to our lives. Whitehead called the Eternal, "Creativity." Every step we take, every act that issues from our being here happens within the field of God. Insofar as we align ourselves with that field, the energy of God flows into the actual living of our lives. Neither evil nor death is a match for the field of God. That is what we mean by the notion of the resurrection. Death may change our form. But remember: Death is an event in time and time is an event within God. Death is the end of time. Death is not the end of life or light. Resurrection means that our lives are ultimately defined more by eternity than by time.

You will recall that I described a person not as an object, but as a "region of behavior." Certainly when I look at you I see a person with definite contours, a shade of hair and eyes, a visible, measurable object. Yet, more strictly speaking, a person does not exist simply as an object in the world. When a person dies, it is their "objectness" that leaves us. Each of us belongs to an interlacing field of relatedness and our individual existences are identifiable extrapolations from that field. We should harken to the reality that every person is more than we can see. The boundaries of our lives are somewhat arbitrary and we have placed far too much stock in the boundary of time. Since we cannot speak outside this boundary, we have to rely on our imagination to take us there. When I ask you who you are, I am usually not referring to the cosmetics of your presence. I am more likely referring to relationships and influences and ideas that have formed you. Similar to the Heisenberg uncertainty principle, uncertainty belongs to the "whoness" and "whereness" of your being here. What you see is never all that you get.

To be sure, then, we are much more than our "objective" selves. To use a much abused phrase, the "original sin" for each of us is the radical localizing of our lives. You have a discernable location and physical dimensions, but they do not either define or fully describe you. You are a constellation of teeming connectivity. What I see when I look at you is simply a localized representation of your relational being in the world. Embrace interdependence.

When we come to the religious conclusion that love is the highest good, we are not simply selecting one value to elevate to a sacred status. Loving springs from accepting and embracing our whole selves. Worship alone cannot confirm our faith. The point of faith is to live out God's presence, to bear God's light in our world. The "big bang" did not happen out there, outside of us. Rather, we began inside the "big bang." Creation is still happening and every creation is an act of light and love. Each of us embodies the primordial energy of God. God is not somewhere else hidden from us; God is right here, hidden within us. Let us regain a sense of wonder. You are God's nearest presence in the world. Each of us is a moment of the Eternal. God is right here in this wonderful, awesome, mysterious world, taking us by surprise.

VIII.

A POSTSCRIPT
LIVING WITH SCIENCE
AND RELIGION

Mystery often creates anxiety, if not outright fear. There are, of course, constructive and destructive responses to fear and anxiety in our lives. There are rational and irrational responses. The irrational and destructive response is to cope with fear by instilling fear in others. That is often what happens when one nation is threatened by the power or the rhetoric of another. The mutualization of fear was the essence of the cold war during the latter half of the 20th century. The East and the West managed an uneasy balance of fear as nuclear arsenals capable of annihilating the other were maintained with poised readiness.

The fear between individuals often leads to less grand, but just as isolating, cold wars between persons. Some people live their lives together with little genuine communication. The fear of the other results in isolation. Furthermore, it is fear masquerading as strength that often creates acts of intimidation, abuse, and even cruelty. The destruction and irrational response to fear can create costly and crippling conditions both for individuals and for nations.

Both science and religions in their highest instincts represent constructive and rational responses to our anxiety-ridden lives. The warring that sometimes erupts between science and religion generally represents the failure to accept the limitations of understanding that belong to our human situation. Religion and science need never be in conflict with one another. Science responds to the unknown and the inexplicable, that persistent a wellspring of anxiety and fear, by mounting rational inquiries into the nature of our world. As I have previously observed, science is continually pushing back the curtains of ignorance. The scientific mind persistently refuses to be intimidated by the unknown and never accepts ignorance as a final answer. Ignorance spawned by the boundaries of the unknown becomes the platform for further inquiry. The scientific mind is bent toward unraveling one more mystery, enlightening one more corner of darkness, overcoming one more avenue of debilitating ignorance.

Science is a humbling inquiry. Every discovery opens up new paths of inquiries. Discovery itself inspires new discoveries and shines a light on the massiveness of what is yet to be known. The pace of learning is accelerated by every new discovery. So, with virtual certainty, humans will learn more in the 21st century than was learned in all human history, including the 20th century. The pace of learning, the pace of gaining understanding is quickening. But the field of the unknown is so enormous that all our accelerating learning will not deplete the mystery in which we exist.

During the 20th century, science was perhaps known best by its achievements in physics. The theories of relativity, the understanding of quantum mechanics and quantum field theory open entirely new horizons of human understanding and present new puzzles to be solved. The new knowledge to be discovered in the world of physics will not slow down. More sophisticated instruments of inquiry continue to be developed and new light on old mysteries will break through. Our grand scientific theories of our universe will likely be modified. New theories of everything will emerge. Science rarely dismantles older theories of the universe or its forces such as gravity and electromagnetism. Rather, it builds new and more comprehensive models for interpreting our universe. The Standard Model of Physics, for example, will surely be superseded by new models that provide greater understanding. After all, we know something about less than 5% of the stuff in our own universe.

The reach of scientific understanding will continue to expand and the enlightening powers of physics in the 20th century will be augmented by our increasingly rapid advancement in biology. The future of life will become a consuming enterprise during this century. The struggle to augment human intelligence, the advances and even the threats of artificial intelligence will escalate as major scientific and moral issues. As never before, human beings have the capacity to manipulate the development of human life with our advancing knowledge of the human genome. We will be able to re-program babies before they are born to modify their genetic structure in order to eliminate specific birth defects and to prevent certain diseases and physical malfunctions from occurring after the child is born.

In addition, such well-known scientists and entrepreneurs such as Stephen Hawking and Bill Gates, Elon Musk and Apple-cofounder, Steve Wozniak were among 2500 co-signers of an open letter expressing alarm over the rising threat of weapons powered by artificial intelligence. The United Nations, for example, is discussing a ban on such weapons. The Future of Life Institute, co-founded by Max Tegmark, a professor at Massachusetts Institute of Technology, has, as one of its purposes, the effort to address the dark side of artificial intelligence. In this century, not the next, we will develop artificial intelligence that is smart enough to power itself and to improve its own software, over and over again, every hour or perhaps every few seconds. It will quickly become smarter than humans and those advances, as Max Tegmark says, "could be wonderful or it could be pretty bad." So, the advance of science, in the near term, cannot only overcome fear and diminish the tragedy of crippling diseases, it can also create fear from developments and advances that exceed our capacity to control the outcome of those advances. The world of science is bringing us new visions of hope and dizzying new horizons of anxiety. We should never be dismayed by the changing views and descriptions of our cosmos. Keep thought alive.

Facing these new horizons, I believe that it is important that we recognize that we live and will continue to live in a world not only fueled by science, but one that is also fueled by religion. Religion, too, must be prepared to change. Religions can become trapped by the barnacles of their own history. The forms of religion can become rigid and immovable. We should keep faith open to new light and higher insight. The energy of God continues to bring new light if our eyes are open. While faith's learning is more episodic than linear, we should keep faith open enough for the energy of God to stir our souls and our faith communities. If we keep faith alive, we may be startled by God's presence in unexpected places and in unsuspecting moments.

Faith and reason will continue to interact on the human stage. We will not come to a time when either reason or faith should be set aside. To live well, as I have stressed throughout this book, we will always need both the scientist and the poet, the thinker and the believer. We will live most fully when the dance of our daily lives embraces the point and counterpoint of faith and reason. It is, I believe, short-sighted and naïve to regard religion as simply a holdover from the ravages of human ignorance. Religion, like science, is about shedding light. Religion also is about vanquishing the arenas of darkness. The human situation will never be made whole by science alone because reason alone will not be sufficient to sustain us. It will require music and art and poetry and myth and faith and reason to be able to live our lives to the fullest. We are not objects in a void. We are relational beings existing in a web of connectivity and interdependence that cannot be described or understood by facts alone. Keep poetry alive.

Living well will not only require knowledge; it will require trust. And in our world of fear and conflict that threatens to overpower reason, trust is in short supply. Above all else, communities of faith should be communities of trust. The interdependent trust which is fashioned by faith communities can become a powerful resource for living in an uncertain world. Science alone will not be able to make us safe from either the darkness of ignorance or the darkness of malice and evil. Relating to another in a way that sees the other as a component of our own being present can bring light into the dark corners of human experience. Science pushes back the boundaries of darkness. Religion engages the darkness. Religion can be a force for dispelling the darkness that sometimes overwhelms our interior lives.

I believe that, in the final analysis, we should applaud and undergird the reformations of life and understanding that are brought to us by science. We need greater understanding, even when what we are learning makes us uneasy. Our religion's embrace, like the embrace of science, needs to become broader and more tolerant. Otherwise, our religions channel fear instead of hope.

Both science and religion bring light into the world. Each scientific discovery brings a shred of new light. And every act of love is an event of light. Each of us is created as a new episode of light in the world. Our high calling is to become a force for bringing hope by letting our light be present. The labors of our disciplined scientific community working along side communities of faith and trust that are echoes of God's presence can constitute the dawning of light in a world that is crippled by ignorance and distrust. Though we may be adrift along the outer regions of our vast galaxy, which we call the Milky Way, each of us can become a tiny ray of light in the vastness of our world. Each of us is a star streaking across our human scene. Every dawning of light matters. Every person's light counts. Our calling is to become the light in the darkness that only each of us can be. Every person's light can illuminate someone's path. Reach out and become somebody's light. Become somebody's hope. As you do, you change the course of the entire universe. God is present in every one of us. Each one of us can become the voice of God in our awesome world. Love lived and hope embodied will be the clearest word from God that somebody has ever experienced.